HOMEGROWN HUMUS

Homegrown
HUMUS

COVER CROPS IN A NO-TILL GARDEN

ANNA HESS

WETKNEE BOOKS

ISBN: 1539179796
ISBN-13: 978-1539179795

Contents

Fall oats make an attractive and vigorous soil cover that naturally dies over the winter in zone 6 and colder.

Introduction

During the last four years that I've experimented with growing cover crops, my garden soil has turned darker and yields of many vegetables have increased dramatically. Both my own honeybees and wild pollinator populations have been boosted by the copious nectar produced by buckwheat plantings, and my chickens have enjoyed the winter greenery from oilseed radish leaves. Plus, having cover crops on the ground during the winter prevents erosion, keeps soil microorganisms humming along, and just makes the garden a more interesting place to be. Nowadays, I can't imagine doing without my beds of buckwheat, radishes, and oats.

Planting cover crops is a quick-and-easy afterthought in my current garden, but it wasn't always that way. I experienced a steep learning curve when I first began growing cover crops in my chemical-free, no-till garden. Most information on growing cover crops is written for people who plow their soil every year and are willing to spray herbicides, and I had some spectacular failures while selecting the cover crop species that would do well without these disturbances.

Buckwheat not only improves your soil, it also feeds honeybees and native pollinators.

Chances are you'll have to experiment as well. The further you live from my zone-6, southwest Virginia garden, or the more your gardening techniques differ from my own, the more of a commitment you'll need to make to figuring out the best way to slide cover crops into your fallow periods. Luckily, experimentation is half the fun, and my experiences should at least help you set off in the right direction, inspiring you to give cover crops a try.

Most cover crops are allowed to grow until they reach full bloom, then are killed.

Choosing the right cover crop

What is a cover crop?

Cover crops are plants purposely sown in the garden to improve the soil's fertility, to fight weeds, to prevent erosion, and to keep the ecosystem in balance. These crops are sometimes known as "green manure," especially if the plants are tilled into the soil. Here, I'll be considering cover crops that can be managed without tilling in.

The list of plants that have been used as cover crops is quite extensive, and even includes common vegetables and flowers like kale and sunflowers. If you want to expand your experiments beyond the species in this book, two good sources of cover crop information include *Managing Cover Crops Profitably*— an extensive document available free at www.sare.org —and Northern Great Plains Research Laboratory's Cover Crop Chart—a simpler document that provides more breadth but less depth and that is available for free download at www.ars.usda.gov/SP2UserFiles/Place/54450000/CC C/CCC_v13_5_2012.pdf. Between those two documents and this book, you should definitely find at least a few plants that match up well with your garden.

Types of cover crops

When choosing cover crops, it's handy to look at broad categories to find out which one (or ones) best fit your needs. The first distinction to consider is whether your plants are annuals (meaning they'll go to seed and die in less than a year) or perennials (meaning they will live for many years). Perennial cover crops have a place in pastures or tilled-garden settings, but, for our purposes, you'll be better off sticking to annuals.

It's also helpful to break cover crops down into two other categories—legumes and non-legumes. Legumes are members of the bean family, and cover-crop legumes include clovers, cowpeas, field peas, vetch, and medics. Legumes differ from most other kinds of plants because they've teamed up with soil bacteria to enable them to pull nitrogen out of the air. As a result, legumes are able to grow in soil that hasn't been recently dosed with manure, compost, or other nitrogen fertilizers, and (when managed correctly) legume cover crops can reduce your need to apply compost to the soil.

Legumes grow bumps on their roots, known as nodules, to house bacteria. The bacteria grab nitrogen out of the air that plants can't usually take in, and in exchange, the plants feed their little friends sugars harvested from the energy of the sun.

Non-legumes include all other types of cover crops, notably grains and crucifers (the latter of which are members of the same family as cabbage and mustard). While legumes can make their own nitrogen and act as quick fertilizers for the soil, non-legumes create more organic matter and enrich the soil longer term.

I'll explain more about how to maximize the amount of organic matter you get from your cover crops in a later section, but for now, it's worth considering why you want to grow cover crops. Are you trying to replace the compost or manure used to fertilize your garden annually? If so, go for legumes. On the other hand, if you're like me and are trying to improve the quality of your garden soil, you'll want to stick to grains and crucifers.

Growing your own organic matter

Why is it so important to increase the organic matter levels of your soil? Organic matter acts like a buffer, evening out all kinds of problematic soil conditions. Soil high in organic matter will suck up excess water during rains without becoming waterlogged, then will let the moisture drip back out to keep plants healthy during ensuing droughts. Organic matter clings to soil nutrients that otherwise might be washed away, and it feeds microorganisms that help your plants. That's why good gardeners crave dark, aerated soil high in organic matter and do everything within their power to increase their organic matter levels over time.

Healthy soil in a no-till garden will be dark and will hold together due to the work of microorganisms.

Unfortunately, if left to its own devices, mainstream agriculture generally decreases the amount of organic matter in the soil every year. Microorganisms slowly break down organic matter into food, some of which they pass on to plants, and this process can lower your organic matter levels very quickly if you add lots of air to your soil by tilling the ground. Although the decomposition process is slower in no-till gardens, even these spots lose organic matter every year unless you add compost or other amendments to top off the soil's organic-matter supply.

Especially in the early years of a garden, it's handy to add a lot more organic matter than the soil will use up that year, since the residual organic matter will stick around and increase the quality of your growing area. While I recommend compost to keep established soil in good condition, you'd have to add quite a lot to bring poor soils up to par, and all that compost-moving will be hard on your back (and probably on your wallet). To boost organic matter levels quickly, sustainable farmers turn to cover crops.

How much organic matter can you add with cover crops? Quite a bit—you'll likely see darkening of your soil within a year or two of including cover crops in your rotation. My favorite cover crops clock in at 6,000 pounds of dry matter per acre (for buckwheat), 8,000 pounds of dry matter per acre (for oats), 11,700 pounds of dry matter per acre (for oilseed radishes), and 10,000 pounds of dry matter per acre (for rye) when grown in optimal conditions. (Sweet potatoes are a less-traditional cover crop, so data on their dry matter accumulation isn't readily available.) The actual amount of organic matter you grow will depend on your soil conditions, but those pounds of organic matter will definitely add up to a healthier garden.

How to kill cover crops

After deciding between growing nitrogen and growing organic matter, the other main factor to consider when choosing cover crops for a no-till garden is—how will you ensure your cover crop doesn't keep growing as a weed and out-compete your vegetables? While you can dig up cover crops or till them in if you're desperate, it's better to choose crops that are easy to kill without disturbing the ground.

If not killed correctly, cover crops can turn into a weed problem in your garden.

In the summer, mowing is the best way to kill cover crops in a no-till garden. Only a few cover crops are easily mow-killed, though, and even with those that mow-kill well, you'll want to plan your garden season so you can allow the crops to reach full bloom (but not set seed) before cutting them down. Depending on the size of your garden, you may use a lawnmower, weed-eater, or scythe to do the mowing, or might simply yank up handfuls then lay the roots on top of the leaves on a sunny day. The latter method is actually my favorite with buckwheat in the summer garden since I can often pull up a bed of buckwheat by hand in the same amount of time it would take to put the blade on my scythe or to get the gas mower started.

My other favorite method of killing cover crops in a no-till garden is to let winter do the work for me. Here's where those of you gardening much further north or south than my zone-6 garden will have to do some experimenting (although *Managing Cover Crops Profitably* does provide zone-related tips on where certain crops will winter-kill). When I plant oilseed radishes and oats in the fall, cold weather naturally wipes out nearly all the plants during the winter, producing a mulch that rots into the soil by early spring (for oilseed radishes) or by early summer (for oats). Later sections will provide planting dates for those of you who want to experiment with winter-killing.

Laying down a kill mulch is a sure-fire way to get rid of cover crops that didn't die when you asked them nicely.

After a month under cardboard and straw, annual ryegrass was fully dead and partially rotted into the soil.

Although mow-killing and winter-killing are my favorite ways to kill cover crops, it's worth having a couple of other techniques up your sleeve in case your experiments don't go as planned. A kill mulch is an easy way to kill just about any plants as long as you have a month or two to wait before planting the next crop. Simply mow your cover crops as close to the ground as you can, lay down corrugated cardboard (being sure to overlap the edges by at least four inches so plants can't sneak up between layers), then top it all off with straw (or another vegetable-garden-appropriate mulch). Lack of sunlight will kill all but the most ornery plants in short order, at which point you can either cut holes in the cardboard to plant directly into the soil, or can move the cardboard to kill mulch a new garden area.

If you don't have time to kill mulch and you really need to get rid of those cover crops, you'll be forced to pull them up by the roots. I actually use this method often with buckwheat, as I mentioned above, but weeding out most other cover crops will be a lesson in patience. Good planning ensures you won't need to pull up cover crops by hand very often.

If all else fails, pull your cover crops up by the roots.

Oilseed radishes reliably winter-kill in zone 6.

My five favorite cover crops

Picking favorites

Although it seems unfair to the many other excellent cover crop species out there, I recommend you at least consider giving my five favorites top billing in your own garden. Buckwheat is an excellent summer cover crop for everyone except those who face an inability to irrigate during hot, dry summers, or for those who have excessively clayey, waterlogged soil. Sweet potatoes are an outside-the-box summer alternative, perfect filler for bare spots in the forest garden where they provide winter mulch and food for the table. Meanwhile, oats and oilseed radishes are top-notch fall cover crops if you live in zone 6 or colder, handling most problematic soil conditions with aplomb. Even if you garden in a warmer area, oilseed radishes would be easy to pull up by hand and are probably worth a try, although I wouldn't recommend oats if you're unable to winter-kill them. Finally, rye is a winter trooper, surviving extreme cold and waterlogged soil to create a dense mulch for your late summer garden.

Along with the profiles of the big five here, I'll share my experiences with several other cover crop species in the next chapter. While the cover crops I consider there didn't make the cut in my own garden, understanding how they grow should make it easy to pick the ones that might work better for you. Chances are good that there is at least one cover crop species that will be a perfect fit for your unique garden, and I'd be willing to bet either buckwheat, sweet potatoes, oats, oilseed radishes, or rye end up being among your favorites.

Buckwheat

Buckwheat (*Fagopyrum esculentum*) is the only summer cover crop I use often in my vegetable garden. Although the plants might need a bit more time when days shorten in the fall, you can grow a bed of buckwheat from seed to mulch in four weeks, and the plants are easy to rip out by hand.

Buckwheat fills quick gaps in the summer garden.

I devote the sunniest part of my garden to spring and fall vegetables, then give that area the summer off by planting back-to-back crops of buckwheat. After the first planting is mature, I scatter new seeds amid the older buckwheat plants just as they bloom, then yank and drop the old plants to form a protective mulch over the soil surface. Within a couple of days, the first round of buckwheat has dried up enough to let the new buckwheat seedlings peek through, and the cycle continues.

Pulled up and left to dry in the summer sun, buckwheat is ready to plant into within a few days.

Even if you don't want to give your garden the whole summer off, you might find a month-long window to let buckwheat grow. Buckwheat is very succulent, so it doesn't tie up nitrogen if you plant into the soil a mere week after mowing the cover crop down. Alternatively, you can yank out whole buckwheat plants and pile them on the edges of the bed to compost, which allows you to plant into the bare soil immediately, then to pull the dried buckwheat plants back around the seedlings a week or two later as mulch.

In addition to fitting well into the summer garden, buckwheat has the benefit of pretty (although small) flowers that pollinators enjoy. In fact, a bed of buckwheat will attract so many pollinating insects that folks scared of bees may want to keep their buckwheat beds a distance from the house. Entomologists, on the other hand, will revel in peering up close at the brilliantly-colored bees and wasps, most of whom won't sting unless severely provoked.

Buckwheat seeds are large, so it's expensive to buy them online, but most feed stores will sell you a 50-pound sack for around $16. We go through about one bag per year, slipping buckwheat into gaps in our gardens and pastures, but you'll probably use considerably less than 50 pounds in a backyard garden. Recommended planting rates for farmers are between 50 and 96 pounds per acre, but I plant much more heavily to ensure buckwheat covers the ground completely and I don't need to weed. If you're spreading buckwheat seeds directly onto the soil surface and want a closed canopy nearly immediately, plan on using about a pound of buckwheat seeds for every 20 to 25 square feet.

Assuming your garden is on the small side, you'll likely have some seeds leftover if you buy your buckwheat in 50-pound sacks. While you can save that seed until next year, it will probably attract weevils, so you'll be better off feeding the excess seed to your chickens or your family after the first fall frost. Be aware that buckwheat seeds are low in protein, roughly equivalent to corn, so they're more of a treat for your flock than a full ration.

Weevils are a problem if you want to store grain seeds for more than a few months. Here, a weevil is hollowing out oat seeds.

Now that I've sung the praises of buckwheat, let's come back down to earth. Buckwheat produces only about 2 to 3 tons of dry matter per acre, which is significantly less than many other cover crops. On the other hand, if you consider that buckwheat produced that much organic matter in only one month, the cover crop still looks pretty good.

However, you'll see much less organic-matter production if you're trying to grow buckwheat in problematic soil. Buckwheat is able to handle soil that's recently been woodland and contains lots of decomposing organic matter, but it's less hardy in compacted or wet ground. Buckwheat also won't handle droughts and dies when touched by frost, making it inappropriate for fall planting and for summers if you don't irrigate. All of that said, if you have at least moderate quality garden soil and water your garden anyway, buckwheat will probably thrive in your summer garden.

Sweet potatoes

Sweet potatoes are an unusual cover crop that provide food as well as produce biomass. In this photo, I've just harvested the bed to the right, piling the vines under the tree, and the bed to the left is yet to be harvested.

I'll admit that the second species on my top-five list is an unusual choice for cover cropping. But sweet potatoes (*Ipomoea batatas*) have proven to be copious biomass-producers, produce edible tubers, can be started at home for free, and provide a living mulch under fruit trees. I now grow sweet potatoes in place of buckwheat in parts of the garden that will be fallow all summer, especially just past the tree root zone in the forest garden.

It's easy to start sweet potato slips at home using a seed flat, sand, and a heat pad.

Sweet potatoes are like buckwheat in that they can't handle even a hint of cold weather, but unlike buckwheat, you do need to plan ahead if you want to have plenty of spare sweet potato slips to fill up your garden. In contrast to most garden vegetables, sweet potatoes aren't started from seed, and you also don't plant chunks of the tubers the way you would with white potatoes. Instead, a bed of sweet potatoes begins with slips—little shoots that come up from the parent tuber, are clipped off, and are induced to root.

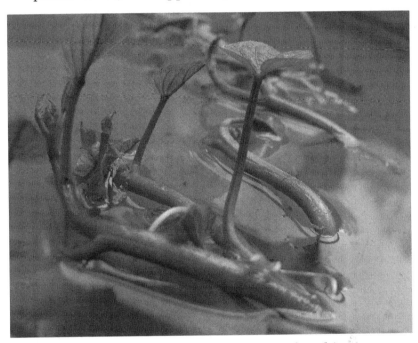

Slips root within a week or two when placed in water.

You can buy slips at garden centers around your frost-free date, but it's much cheaper to start your own from store-bought or home-grown sweet potatoes. We haven't bought sweet potato slips since 2008, making this species our cheapest cover crop. Each year, we begin with about six skinny tubers on April 1, sinking each one halfway into a flat of moist creek gravel. (Sand will work too.) A heat pad underneath the flat is essential to get the sweet potatoes off to a good start, and a clear plastic cover helps keep moisture in until the sprouts begin to appear.

Once sprouts are about three inches long, you can easily snap each one off the tuber. But be patient—if you put tubers in a flat on April 1, you might not see any sprouts long enough to remove until May 1. After they start growing, though, sprouts will come fast and furious.

Sprouts excised from the tuber need to go through a rooting stage before you put them in the garden. Sink the bottom half of the slip in water and let the container sit on a sunny windowsill for a week or two until at least three roots per slip are at least an inch long.

Now your slips are ready to be set out into the garden. Sink the slip up to its leaves in the soil, water well, and repeat watering as necessary until the plants take hold (usually less than a week).

After that, the sky's the limit. One sweet potato slip will quickly spread out for more than three feet in every direction, completely covering the soil surface. My favorite use for sweet potato cover crops is in the forest garden between young fruit trees, where the sweet potatoes suppress weeds beyond the trees' root zone, while also providing a living mulch beneath the canopy. Although sweet potatoes will send out small adventitious roots along their vines' length, those don't seem to compete much with the tree roots. (The tubers *can* attract voles that will go on to nibble on your tree roots though, so be forewarned!)

The best time to plant sweet potato slips is between your frost-free date (May 15 here) and two weeks later, but slips will still create appreciable biomass (if much smaller tubers) when planted later. In fact, setting out late slips is how I realized sweet potatoes were a good tool to have in my cover-crop arsenal—even slips planted in early July made lots of leaves and stems.

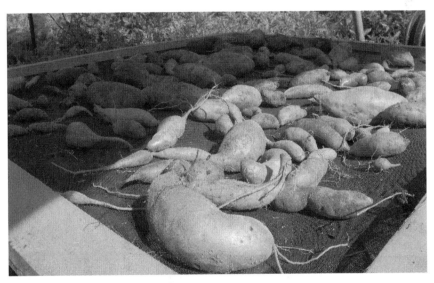

Curing sweet potatoes.

If you don't want to harvest the roots, you can just let frosts naturally kill the sweet potato vines, but why waste such a yummy addition to your Thanksgiving dinner? To harvest the tubers, you'll want to head out to the garden at least a couple of weeks before your first frost. I usually cut the vines near the ground with pruning clippers, then pile the plant matter around the base of my trees as a rich winter mulch. Next, I dig each clump of sweet potatoes with a spade, being careful not to cut into the tubers. After digging, sweet potatoes need to cure for 2 weeks at 80 to 85 degrees Fahrenheit, during which time starches turn into sugars and improve the flavor of the vegetables. Later, the potatoes will keep all winter on a dry kitchen shelf.

Since sweet potatoes are usually grown as a vegetable rather than as a cover crop, I can't find any solid data on organic-matter accumulation for the species. However, they've become an indispensable part of my forest-gardening campaign and I highly recommend you give them a try as well.

Expensive seeds are the only disadvantage of planting oilseed radishes. In 2012, I paid $3.50 per pound for a 25-pound bag once I factored in shipping costs.

Oilseed radishes

Oilseed radishes (*Raphanus sativus*) only have one major downside—the seeds are expensive and usually have to be ordered online. If you're willing to pay the price, though, the plants will definitely improve your garden soil.

When hunting for radish seeds, you should be aware of the many different common names that refer to the same plant—tillage radish, oilseed radish, groundhog radish, fodder radish, and forage radish. Daikon radishes are subtly different, having been selected for palatability to humans, but will work too if you have a cheap seed source. (And, as my mother and sister attest, you can also eat the tubers of cover-crop radishes, although they're not as delectable as true daikon radishes.) The small, red radishes you may already grow in your garden as a vegetable are different and are unlikely to produce nearly as much biomass.

Oilseed radishes develop large tubers that break up hardpan.

No matter what they're called, radish cover crops should be planted in late summer, a bit earlier than you'd plant grains for winter cover. Here in zone 6, we seed oilseed radishes between August 1 and September 7, fitting them into gaps in the vegetable garden as space becomes available. You'll get the most biomass production from plants seeded at the early end of that planting window, but beds planted in early September make a good stand for us in most years.

Thick planting in a no-till garden costs a bit more in seed but saves time.

As usual, I plant much more thickly than the seeding rates used by conventional farmers. On large farms, oilseed radishes are drilled into the soil at a rate of 12 to 20 pounds per acre, but I scatter seeds thickly at about 530 pounds per acre (or a pound for every 80 square feet), ensuring that the leaves quickly cover the ground and shade out any weeds.

Fall-planted oilseed radishes can provide a winter pick-me-up when chickens have run out of other greenery.

Visitors to my fall garden are always drawn to the yellow-green oilseed radish beds and ask if they can have a taste—the verdict is that the plants aren't very flavorful but are definitely beautiful. Our chickens disagree, chowing down on the leaves repeatedly until there's nothing left except tubers and stems. While you won't put quite as much organic matter into the soil if you let your chickens eat the radish tops, stacking chickens and cover crops can be a good way to provide both nitrogen and organic matter to the soil while keeping your flock healthy at a difficult time of year.

It's the tubers that are doing most of the work in the garden. Oilseed radishes are given the name "tillage radish" for their ability to push through compacted layers of soil, breaking up hardpans and letting later crops enjoy more wiggle room around their roots. Once the radish plants are winter-killed (around 25 degrees Fahrenheit), their roots rot into the soil, leaving behind organic matter, channels for water and air to move through, and food for earthworms.

Worms are attracted to the decomposing tubers in early spring.

Despite their size, radish roots quickly dissolve into the soil.

After winter-killing, both leaves and tubers rot quickly, leaving the soil bare and ready for spring planting well before our frost-free date. In fact, if I'm not going to be planting early-spring crops into oilseed-radish beds, I usually top the ground off with straw in February or March to prevent weeds from growing. Otherwise, I plant directly into the debris— radishes don't hold onto nitrogen like woodier cover crops, so there's no need to wait long after the radishes die before seeding vegetables in their place.

Oats are a productive fall cover crop that leave a straw-like mulch on the ground until mid-spring.

Oats

When every dollar counts, oats (*Avena sativa*) become the fall cover-crop winner. A 50-pound bag of oat seeds purchased at the feed store costs about $16 and seeds roughly 1,080 square feet at my profligate planting rates of about a pound for every 25 square feet. In contrast, conventional farmers use 96 to 128 pounds of oat seeds per acre, which cuts costs much further, but lets a lot of weeds through.

Oat seeds can be bought cheaply in bulk at our local feed store.

Oats can be planted directly into a lawn in late summer. This method, developed by Colin Seis and Darryl Cluff, is known as pasture cropping. To grow oats in a pasture or lawn, first sprinkle the seeds amid the grasses, then weed-eat the plant matter down as close to the ground as possible. If your patch is located in full sun, you'll see strong growth of the oats equivalent to the same cover crop planted in a bare garden bed.

Fall-planted oats grow three or four feet tall, then naturally winter-kill in zone 6 and colder (and even in much of zone 7), leaving a straw-like mulch that holds the soil mostly weed-free until the middle of May. That mulch can be raked back for direct-seeded crops, or pulled up around transplants immediately. While I like to sow oilseed radishes in parts of the garden that will be planted in carrots, peas, and other spring crops, I prefer oats as a cover crop in garden areas that won't be planted until after the frost-free date.

As with oilseed radishes, choosing the right planting time is critical. In my zone-6 garden, I plant oats between August 1 and September 15, meaning that oats can handle slightly later planting than oilseed radishes. Similarly, oats can handle wetter soil than my other cover crops, and will thrive in my worst, waterlogged-clay garden area.

I've even had luck tossing oat seeds onto patches of semi-bare lawn in August. The oats came up and produced biomass that helped shade out grasses in an area that was going to be kill-mulched into vegetable-garden production the next spring. Similarly, old farming manuals suggest planting fall oats amid strawberry plants to grow your own mulch, but my one experiment with this technique resulted in low berry yields the next spring. If you've had better luck with this companion planting, I hope you'll report back so I can tell later readers how to enjoy the best of both worlds.

This picture, taken in late April, shows why rye is one of my new favorite cover crops. It holds the soil over the winter, grows quickly in the spring, and can withstand (and even thrive in) waterlogged soil.

Rye

When I published the first edition of *Homegrown Humus*, my cover-crop campaign had a gap in the early spring. Oats and oilseed radishes were good fall cover crops, but both died by midwinter, leaving nothing to grow until buckwheat-planting season, which begins after the frost-free date. And then I found rye.

Rye is more winter hardy than any of the other commonly-planted grain cover crops.

Annual rye (*Secale cereale*) is the most winter-hardy of all commonly-grown grains, with plants establishing when sown as late as the middle of November. This makes it easy to slip rye into beds that open up after you dig fall carrots and after the first frost nips your tomatoes. Plus, if you plant your oats a little too early and that cover crop starts to bloom, it's simple to scatter rye seeds amid the oat stalks, mow the oats to the ground, and watch a second round of biomass-building happen during the same fall season.

To add to their positive traits, rye seedlings don't just sprout and wait until spring either—the plants continue to grow (albeit slowly) during warm days throughout the winter, reaching a height of perhaps three to five inches by early spring. The winter growth keeps most weeds in check, a major bonus if you're trying to keep chickweed and dead nettle out of your garden. Then the rye cover crop really takes off with the first hint of warm weather, and can produce up to 10,000 pounds of dry matter per acre before being mow-killed at full bloom.

Rye in bloom.

Rye is easy to kill by cutting to the ground just after it reaches full bloom.

Our rye bloomed by the book, just as day length achieved 14 hours. (You can insert your latitude into the calculator at http://astro.unl.edu/classaction/animations/coordsm otion/daylighthoursexplorer.html to learn when your location will achieve a day length of 14 hours in the spring.) That bloom time happily coincided with our frost-free date, allowing us to cut the rye to the ground at the same time we were planting frost-sensitive crops elsewhere. As long as we were careful to wait until full bloom and to mow the rye precisely to ground level (a weed-eater worked well), every rye plant died on schedule.

Rye stubble is high in carbon, so you'll need to wait a while before planting into the cover crop, unless you apply extra nitrogen.

However, rye does have a caveat. Since the plants are higher in carbon than many other cover crops, they will actually steal nitrogen from young seedlings if you plant into the stubble less than three weeks after mow-killing. You can either wait out that period and use your rye beds for midsummer plantings of fall vegetables, or you can add extra nitrogen in the form of compost or urine around seedlings transplanted into the rye stubble. (Be sure to water urine down to one part urine in eight parts water if applying around living plants.) It's also worth noting that rye is reputed to have allelopathic qualities that will prevent small-seeded vegetable from sprouting, so you'll want to wait a full month before direct-seeding plants like carrots or lettuce into beds that had recently grown rye.

As long as you give your rye beds the required rest period before replanting, you'll find rye is a workhorse in the winter and early spring garden. And the seeds are available at most feed stores, meaning their price is quite low, comparable to the price of oats and buckwheat. We now plant rye by the fifty-pound bag every year and appreciate the nearly-free straw we grow in our garden.

Rye seeds are inexpensive and easily available at our local feed store.

In general, I don't repeat plantings of cover crops that allow weeds to poke through and don't create appreciable biomass.

Cover crops that didn't make the cut

The road less traveled by

Every garden is a little different, and the cover crops that fit the bill in my garden might not be perfect for yours. That's why I'm giving a brief rundown in this chapter of cover crops that nearly worked for me—they might be just your cup of tea.

Sunflowers

Sunflowers (*Helianthus annuus*) will be a good fit if you need your cover crop patch to look like a flower garden, especially if you don't mind doing some weeding. Lets start with the positives. Sunflowers pull up nutrients from deep in the soil, perhaps because they're good at teaming up with arbuscular mycorrhizae (beneficial soil fungi), and sunflowers are great for attracting pollinators. The plants also produce sunflower seeds, which can feed you or your chickens if the wild birds don't eat them first.

Where sunflowers fall down on the job is keeping weeds at bay. You'll need to either weed around the base of your sunflowers or mulch the plants, and my goal with cover crops is to make them take work away from the vegetable garden, not add to it. I've had some success with growing buckwheat under rows of sunflowers, but the method is a bit more tricky than growing buckwheat on its own since you need to harvest and replant the buckwheat a few times over the course of the sunflowers' growing cycle, and the big sunflower stems get in the way.

I haven't found any data on how much organic matter sunflowers produce per acre, but my gut feeling is that they make less than the buckwheat I could have grown in the bed during the same time period. Sunflower stems are too big and woody to break down quickly into mulch, so you'll probably need to cut them up and add them to the compost pile. In the end, I consider sunflowers worth growing if you want the seeds, but they have not been a quality cover crop in my garden.

Sunflowers attract pollinators and make edible seeds, but don't match up to buckwheat in terms of weed control and biomass production.

Annual ryegrass

Annual ryegrass (*Lolium multiflorum*) looks a lot like a lush lawn, and you'll have the same issues with ryegrass as a cover crop that you might have with lawn grasses—they're both very tough to kill. I decided to give annual ryegrass a try in a waterlogged part of my garden since the cover crop is reputed to produce more biomass than other plants in wet soil. The goal was to repeatedly mow the ryegrass beds down to four inches several times over the course of the growing season, a management strategy that is reputed to produce up to 9,000 pounds of organic matter per acre per year.

Annual ryegrass produces copious organic matter, but is very hard to kill.

Annual ryegrass produces a strong network of roots close to the soil surface.

I was very pleased with ryegrass's ability to colonize and thrive in my worst garden soil, and the lush green grass was very pretty in my spring garden. Even though our lawnmower doesn't cut as high as four inches, the plants still sprang back from repeated mowing, and the tops quickly rotted into the soil and stimulated more growth.

The trouble came when I wanted to rotate the beds out of cover crops and back into vegetables. Annual ryegrass refused to die until I laid down a full kill mulch consisting of a layer of corrugated cardboard topped by straw. An experimental treatment that left out the cardboard layer was less effective.

And after all that effort, the ryegrass didn't seem to have added much organic matter to the soil. As I'll explain in a later chapter, the high-nitrogen leaves rotted quickly into the soil rather than slowly decaying into humus, so little was left behind.

In the end, the only place I'd recommend planting annual ryegrass in a no-till situation is in a temporary pasture. Even there, our chickens weren't nearly as fond of ryegrass as they were of oilseed radishes, although other livestock will probably behave differently.

Barley is more winter-hardy than oats, but less so than rye.

Barley

Barley (*Hordeum vulgare*) fits into the annual-ryegrass category of bad behavior—the plants are tough to kill. I tried out barley hoping it would fill a niche left empty by oats and oilseed radishes, which can only be planted through early September in our area. Barley is more winter hardy, so I got away with scattering seeds in late October and still produced a moderate stand before winter hit.

The bad news with grains more winter hardy than oats is that they also don't die on their own during the cold months. Pulling up barley by hand is far more difficult than yanking out buckwheat—I recommend the latter but not the former. Instead, the preferred no-till method of killing barley is to wait until the plants are in full bloom, then cut them at the base, but that only works if you don't need that garden spot until mid- to late-spring. I ended up kill mulching my barley bed to work the plants into the soil sooner.

Austrian winter peas

Austrian winter peas are a variety of field peas (*Pisum sativum* subsp. *arvense*) that winter-kill readily here in zone 6. The legume is usually mixed with a grain to give the winter peas something to grow up, so

I trialed Austrian winter peas by commingling them with a fall planting of oats.

Austrian winter peas weighed down my oats and made the homegrown mulch decompose too quickly.

Although Austrian winter peas grew and died well in our garden, I seemed to get less out of the beds with a mixture of peas and oats than out of the beds growing oats alone. The peas yanked the oats down prematurely, and the high-nitrogen pea leaves prompted the oats to decompose rapidly. The result was a weed problem in early spring since I'd counted on the oats to keep the bare soil covered until our frost-free date.

Meanwhile, our chickens ignored the Austrian winter peas I'd planted in the pasture, preferring mustard and oilseed radishes. Again, your experience with other types of livestock may be different, and Austrian winter peas are at least a harmless addition to the zone-6, no-till garden, especially if you want to grow nitrogen rather than organic matter.

Crimson clover doesn't put out much growth until spring, so the cover crop can't be counted on as a winter weed suppressor.

Crimson clover

Crimson clover (*Trifolium incarnatum*) is one of the few annual clovers, so I thought I'd give it a try in my garden. Unfortunately, the species had very little going for it. Crimson clover seedlings got a light foothold in my fall garden when planted in early October, but waited to put out much growth until spring. As a result, the beds filled up with winter weeds—just what I was trying to avoid.

Crimson-clover flowers are very attractive to people, but only moderately attractive to pollinators.

The primary reason I planted crimson clover in my garden was to test the claims that pollinators are extremely fond of the flowers. When the plants bloomed in late April, the beds were indeed abuzz...but I soon realized most of the bees were visiting the purple dead nettle and other weeds growing between the crimson-clover plants. A few native bees did visit the crimson clover, but not enough to make it worth my while.

Crimson clover is extremely painful to pull up by hand, but I have read reports that the plants mow-kill readily at bloom, which coincides with my spring planting time. In my father's zone 7 garden, he allows crimson clover to go to seed, at which point it dies naturally, then he plants into the stubble and enjoys self-sowed crimson clover the next fall. If you're looking for a very pretty spring cover crop and don't mind weeding around it, crimson clover might fit into your garden.

Cowpeas

Cowpeas (*Vigna unguiculata*) are summer legumes that fill a similar niche as buckwheat—in fact, you can grow the two mixed together. I'll admit that I didn't give cowpeas an entirely fair shake since the local feed store doesn't sell the seeds, so I had to order them at much greater expense online. That said, I feel that buckwheat fills our summer niche better for a variety of reasons. First, buckwheat matures much faster, so I'm able to slip a round of buckwheat into much shorter gaps in the garden cycle. Second, buckwheat breaks down into a quality mulch much more quickly, meaning there's less of a wait after killing the cover crop before it's safe to plant your vegetables. Finally, cowpeas aren't as easy as they could be to kill.

Cowpeas are woodier than buckwheat, take longer to grow, are harder to kill, and their seeds are more expensive.

Ripping up a mixture of buckwheat and cowpeas killed the buckwheat, but many cowpeas rerooted and kept growing.

I've tried two different techniques for killing cowpeas, and haven't been entirely thrilled by either. Since cowpeas have more tenacious roots than buckwheat, I attempted mow-killing first. Unfortunately, even if you wait until the cowpeas are in bloom, they have a tendency to resprout from the base. My next trial was to yank the cowpeas up by the roots, a technique that is tougher for cowpeas than it is for buckwheat, but easier than for crimson clover, barley, or annual ryegrass. But even after I got them out of the ground, the uprooted cowpeas dried slowly in the summer sun and many rerooted if I didn't flip the plants over a few times during the ensuing days.

All of those negatives aside, I was impressed by the amount of biomass produced by cowpeas, so I might consider trying them again if I had a cheap source of seeds. I suspect cowpeas would shine in longer summer gaps where they can be allowed to achieve their full potential, then could be given a few weeks to rot before planting the fall garden.

Beautiful flowers are just about all sunn hemp has going for it.

Sunn hemp

Sunn hemp (*Crotalaria juncea*) is a frost-sensitive legume that can grow up to eight feet tall in one summer. According to the literature, you can choose to cut the plants at 60 days as a high-nitrogen addition to the compost pile, or you can wait a few more weeks until carbon levels rise and sunn hemp becomes a quality mulch. You can also cut the plants when they're only four feet tall, netting an early harvest, then watch the plants resprout and produce even more biomass. Finally, sunn hemp has been reported to lower populations of soil nematodes, a problematic garden pest.

Unfortunately, sunn hemp failed the two primary tests I throw at summer cover crops—can they produce more biomass than buckwheat and can they suppress weeds? In poor soil (especially in waterlogged areas), the sunn hemp cover crop failed miserably, and even in high-quality garden spots, sunn hemp didn't cover the ground quickly, so weeds grew up among the cover-crop stems. And, to add insult to injury, after devoting precious garden space to sunn hemp all summer, I felt like I got less biomass production from those spots than if I'd planted back-to-back buckwheat for the same period.

Meanwhile, other problems surrounded my experimental sunn hemp planting. I was given the seeds of the variety Tropic Sunn by Harvey Ussery, who was coordinating a test for the Molokai seed company. If I'd wanted to buy more seeds, though, they would have been pricey—$5 per pound, plus shipping. As another negative, sunn hemp looked like it would increase the pressure of a problematic pest— the Japanese beetle—in my garden since the insects flocked to the cover crop and would presumably increase their populations if I didn't devote the time to hand-picking them.

Chickens graze behind young sunn hemp plants in late July. This part of the forest garden is also home to comfrey (in the background) and sweet potatoes (in the foreground).

As with other cover crops that failed on my farm, I suspect sunn hemp has a niche in specific gardens. Bill Mollison sings the praises of sunn hemp in his books, perhaps because his long, dry Australian summers give sunn hemp time to fully prove itself. And even though sunn hemp seeds are currently expensive in the U.S., if the species becomes more popular and prices drop, it might be worth using sunn hemp in areas where you want to plant a crop once and forget it for the entire summer. I accidentally grew sunn hemp together with sweet potatoes in 2013, and the polyculture worked very well—the sweet potatoes covered the ground and prevented weeds from forming, while the sunn hemp took advantage of the rootless soil and empty air space above and below the living mulch. I'll be curious to hear if you use sunn hemp in your garden and find a niche that makes the species worth the price tag.

Cover crop mixtures

Another experiment you might want to consider is mixing multiple types of cover crops together. Various sources suggest you may be able to build a more well-rounded soil and attract more pollinators with cover-crop combinations than with any single species planted alone.

Although his large Austrian homestead is far different from the average, no-till garden in an American backyard, Sepp Holzer's cover-crop experiments are worth a mention in this context. Holzer seeds a wide variety of plants into new ground, then leaves the plot alone for two or three years, finally turning pigs into the pasture to eat down encroaching woody plants. Species Holzer's cover-crop mixtures include sunflowers, hemp, cornflowers, yarrow, calendula, golden marguerites, scented mayweed, spreading bellflowers, comfrey, peas, beans, clover, lupin, cabbages, oilseed rape, turnips, sunflowers, buckwheat, and sweet clover. Later, once the ground has been turned into pastures, he adds in a mixture of grains, legumes, and root crops (turnips, radishes, salsify, black salsify, and Jerusalem artichokes) to feed his cattle and pigs over the winter with no work on his part.

Closer to home, Iowa-based soil-consultant Karl Dallefeld uses mixtures of cover crops to build soil in traditionally-tilled farmland. His recommendations for different soil conditions include:

Scavenging nitrogen - rye, sorghum-sudangrass, radish, rapeseed, ryegrass

Nitrogen fixation - legumes (especially clovers)

Quick spring cover - buckwheat, sorghum-sudangrass, berseem clover, medic

Late-planted winter cover - annual ryegrass, rye, oats, radish, rape, turnips

Erosion control - barley, rye, sorghum-sudangrass, cowpeas

Building soil - rye, sorghum-sudangrass, sweet clover, woollypod and hairy vetch

Loosening compacted soil - radish

Suppressing nematodes - crucifers (only if tilled in)

Dealing with high pH - mustard, berseem clover, ryegrass, vetch

Fighting weeds - rye, oats, buckwheat, radish, berseem clover, chickling and other vetches, cowpeas, subclover

Quick, temporary pastures - annual ryegrass, oats, wheat, sorghum-sudangrass, berseem clover, crimson clover, white clover, red clover

In general, Dallefeld recommends mixtures that include at least one legume, one grass, and one non-legume forb (a category that includes everything that's neither grass nor legume) in each plot. For example, he might plant mustard, berseem clover, ryegrass, and a vetch all at once, figuring that the clover and vetch will add nitrogen to the soil, the mustard will feed pollinators and reduce the number of nematodes, and the ryegrass will build organic matter.

While cover-crop combinations are intriguing, I recommend watching your step when following in Holzer's or Dallefeld's footsteps if you're committed to no-till gardening. Mixtures of multiple species require much more careful management if you want to kill your cover crops without tilling them in, and it's usually a good idea not to let cover crops go to seed if you don't want to end up with extra weed pressure. That said, I think there's plenty of room for experimentation with more diverse no-till cover-crop assemblages, and I hope you'll drop me an email at anna@kitenet.net if you develop systems that work well in your garden. I'll be sure to include your experiences on my blog at http://www.waldeneffect.org/tag/cover_crop/.

Hiding the seeds from birds is one of the most important tricks when planting cover crops.

Growing cover crops

Finding cover crop seeds

I've alluded to much of this planting information in previous sections, but I thought I'd sum it all up to give you a more solid idea of how to manage cover crops in a no-till garden. First, of course, you'll need to hunt down the seeds, and your local feed store should be your initial stop. (By "feed store," I mean a farm-supply company, such as Southern States, although I tend to prefer the smaller, non-chain co-ops.) Asking which cover-crop seeds are available is a good way of finding out what your neighbors grow, but keep in mind that most of those neighbors probably till their soil. Many small feed stores will be willing to break apart a large sack of seed to sell you just a few pounds, but others (especially the chains) are more likely to require that you buy a full 50 pounds.

If your feed store doesn't offer the cover crop seeds you want to try, an online company is sure to fill the gap. The issue to keep in mind here is shipping, since these tacked-on costs will often raise prices to astronomical levels. In my own research, Johnny's Selected Seeds (www.johnnyseeds.com) has good rates and a good selection, although the seeds are still going to cost three to five times as much as they might at your local feed store.

Finally, if buying cover crops in bulk, you'll need to keep storage in mind. I've been guilty of leaving fifty-pound bags of oats and rye sitting on the front porch all summer, with disastrous consequences. As I mentioned previously, weevils like to live in grain seeds, but the worse problem is that mice and rats will also take up residence. A junked freezer or metal trash can are good mouse-proof options for storing large quantities of seed.

Planting cover crops in a no-till garden

The next step is planting. After choosing the right planting window, you'll need to decide whether pinching pennies or keeping work to a minimum is more important to you. As you've probably noticed, I seed much more heavily than the commonly-recommended rates since using extra seed allows me to simply rake back the mulch and scatter seeds directly onto the soil surface. A sprinkle of straw on top keeps the seeds moist in warm weather and prevents birds from stealing grain seeds. Before long, a thick sward springs up and shades out weeds, so I don't do any work after planting, except for killing buckwheat and rye and harvesting sweet potatoes.

Oat seeds come up well when covered by a thin coating of straw.

Radish seeds are too spicy to be appealing to local wildlife, so I simply scatter the seeds on moist soil and do nothing else when planting. You can also often get away with planting rye seeds with no straw cover since this appears to be the least-tasty grain from a wildlife standpoint.

On the other hand, it might be worth your while to take a little more care in planting if your seed is very expensive. In that case, after pulling back the mulch, you'll want to rake about half an inch of topsoil to the side for the entire bed. Scatter seeds much more lightly than I recommend in previous sections (using traditional guidelines instead), then pull the soil over top with the rake, or sift it between your fingers to create an even coating. When planting cover crop seeds sparingly, you may also want to weed once to prevent unintended wild plants from taking over the bed.

Some cover crops break down faster than others after killing. For example, buckwheat (on the left) rots much faster than cowpeas (on the right).

C:N ratios

Unlike vegetables, which usually need some care throughout their lives, cover crops fend for themselves after planting. In hot, dry summers, buckwheat will do better if watered along with your vegetable garden, but there's no need to fertilize or weed in nearly all cases. When the time comes, kill your cover crop using the methods outlined in the "How to kill cover crops" section, then decide how long you need to wait before planting the next round of crops.

Long-time gardeners are probably aware that high-carbon amendments, like wood chips, can steal nitrogen out of the soil, and newly-killed cover crops can have a similar (although less detrimental) effect. The length of time you should wait before planting into cover crops will depend on those plants' C:N ratio. I explain this concept in much greater depth in *Weekend Homesteader: May*, but the gist is that this number is simply the ratio of the amount of carbon to the amount of nitrogen in the plant. Plants high in carbon are woodier and break down more slowly (and have a higher C:N), while plants low in carbon are succulent, break down quickly, and have a low C:N.

In general, substances with a C:N of 10:1 make nitrogen available to plants immediately, while those with a C:N below 25:1 or 30:1 are unlikely to slow down crops planted into the residue. On the other hand, a C:N greater than 30:1 is a sign that you need to give the cover crop a few weeks to mellow out (during which time the C:N will drop) before planting into the improved soil. The table on the following page shows the C:N ratio for several cover crops:

	C:N at kill stage
Legumes	
Field peas:	
Leaves	13 to 25
Stems	27 to 83
Roots	17 to 27
Crimson clover	21
Cowpeas	18 to 22
Non-legumes	
Oilseed radishes:	
Roots	20 to 30
Shoots	10 to 20
Buckwheat:	
Leaves	8 to 10
Stems	12 to 32
Roots	28 to 47
Oats	18 to 25
Annual ryegrass	14 to 40
Sunflowers:	
Leaves	11 to 14
Flowers	14 to 19
Stems	41 to 46
Roots	50 to 68
Rye (at full bloom)	37

Based on this chart (and on my own experience), a week or two is plenty of waiting time after killing buckwheat or legumes, but woodier cover crops like rye will benefit from a three- or four-week fallow period. If you don't want to wait, one option is to pull the cover crops up by their roots and pile them on the sides of the bed, which allows you to plant immediately into the bare soil, then to pull the partially-decomposed cover crops back around the seedlings as mulch a week or two later. You can also add extra compost and transplant directly into root stubble since the high-nitrogen compost will counteract the high-carbon roots until the latter have decomposed and allowed nitrogen to once again become available.

The C:N ratio is important not only when planning rest periods between cover crops and vegetables, but also if your goal is to maximize the amount of long-term organic matter in your soil. In the latter case, though, high C:N ratios are handy rather than harmful. Plants with a high C:N ratio not only rot slowly, they also develop into more permanent humus, so it's worth dealing with longer wait periods if your goal is to improve your soil. With this in mind, you can tweak the C:N ratio of your cover crops not only through species selection, but also by choosing when to kill your plants—waiting until the plants have begun to flower usually means they have added more lignin to their stems, have a higher C:N ratio, and will create more long-lasting humus.

Our garden near the end of August 2011 had cover crops in any empty bed. The result of this method is that about a quarter of the garden is growing organic matter at any given time.

The cover crop year

Even if you allot absolutely no extra growing area to cover crops, chances are you can slide them into gaps and grow an appreciable amount of organic matter. I didn't expand my garden after learning about cover crops, but I soon found I could fit buckwheat and sweet potatoes into summer gaps and oats, rye, and oilseed radishes into winter gaps without taking away space from my vegetables. In fact, as organic matter levels increased in my garden beds, I realized I was getting higher yields from the plots in vegetable production, and was able to cut back my planting area and grow more cover crops. The cycle of soil improvement continues.

In your own garden, I recommend starting small until you learn the intricacies of each cover-crop species you're using. Once you settle on a few species that work for you, you'll become adept at keeping an eye out for garden areas going to waste. Did your cucumbers succumb to blight a month before you'd planned to pull them out and seed fall carrots? A perfect opportunity for a round of buckwheat! Is a bed of green beans eaten up by potato beetles? Go ahead and pull it out and plant some oilseed radishes for winter biomass accumulation.

As you add cover crops to your planting cycle, you'll probably begin to see improvements in your garden ecosystem that far exceed the effects of organic-matter accumulation. I've noticed that spring seedlings seem to be healthier in beds that have grown oats or oilseed radishes over the winter than in beds that have simply been mulched with straw. Perhaps the reason is that the living soil web—microorganisms that feed on the sugars put off by plant roots and, in return, provide micronutrients to the plants—is heartier in beds where something has been green and growing recently. Or maybe the effect is the result of sulfur-related compounds emitted by radishes that kill nematodes and other bad microorganisms in the soil. The increase in pollinators around the farm as a result of buckwheat flowers is easier to decipher, but who knows how many other relationships like this are active in the garden ecosystem while being invisible to our untrained eyes?

Finding the best cover crops to fit into your unique homestead ecosystem is an ongoing endeavor.

As much as I've enjoyed my cover crop journey over the last few years, I'm sure I still have a lot to learn. Are there cover crops chickens will enjoy even more than oilseed radishes? Can I close the homestead fertility loop by growing my own straw and compost in addition to using my current, simple methods of increasing organic matter right in the garden beds?

I'll post updates at on my blog at http://www.waldeneffect.org/tag/cover_crop/ when these questions (and others) have been answered, so I hope you'll email me at anna@kitenet.net if you have experiences to share. In the meantime, let's plant some cover crops and grow some humus!

About the author

Anna Hess lives with her husband Mark Hamilton (plus two spoiled cats, a hard-working dog, two goats, and a varying number of chickens and honeybees) on 58 acres of swamp and wooded hillsides in the mountains of southwest Virginia. The duo spends most of their time homesteading—Anna likes to putter around the garden while Mark uses his inventive streak to build chicken coops and deer deterrents out of a handful of screws and whatever is lying around in the barn. They make a living selling POOP-free chicken waterers (www.AvianAquaMiser.com), writing books (www.Wetknee.com), and blogging about their adventures (www.WaldenEffect.org).

In addition to this title, Anna is the author of dozens of homesteading how-to guides. Of these, *The Weekend Homesteader*, *The Naturally Bug-Free Garden*, *Trailersteading*, and *The Ultimate Guide to Soil* are available on paper, while the rest are ebook-only at this time.

To learn more about Anna's books, visit www.Wetknee.com. While you're there, don't forget to sign up for her email list so you can be alerted when new books are published and when ebooks are free on Amazon. As a thank you, you'll also be given a free copy of *Best Books for Homesteaders*.

Other books you may enjoy

Homegrown Humus is the first book in the Permaculture Gardener series. Don't miss these other titles, full of tips on easy ways to create a healthy garden ecosystem that nourishes the gardener and the ecosystem alike:

The Naturally Bug-Free Garden: "This is the place to start if you are looking for guidance on chemical free gardening." --- Ashley Fishbein

The Ultimate Guide to Soil: "Real techniques for real people." --- Amazon Customer

Index

Made in the USA
Middletown, DE
16 July 2022